Proverbs 1:7 -

"The fear of the Lord is the beginning of knowledge: but fools despise wisdom and instruction. My (daughter) hear the instruction of thy father, and forsake not the law of thy mother: For they shall be an ornament of grace unto thy head, and chains about thy neck."

A Girl's Must-Have Pearls

© 2023 Maureen Thompson All rights reserved

No part of this book may be reproduced or transmitted by any means or in any form, including photocopying or mechanical, or by any information storage or retrieval system, without prior written permission from the author.

Warning: reading or listening to any of the content in this book could have a dramatic and life-changing positive effect on you and your future decision-making. For this miracle, the author can take no credit!

TABLE OF CONTENTS

Foreword by Pastor RC Blakes	4
Acknowledgements	5
Introduction	6
1 The Golden Afro	7
2 Whoa! Wait...What?	9
3 I Wish I Knew When I Was You	11
4 Black Pearl	14
5 Clown With A Crown	16
6 Queens of Colour	18
7 Baby Girl	20
8 Daddy's Girl	23
9 Father Wound	26
10 A Good Man	28
11 Long Live The Queen!	30
12 Mum	32
13 Don't Get Caught A' Bush!	34
14 Betrayed	37
15 A Good Man Lost	39

TABLE OF CONTENTS (CONT.)

16 What Is Wrong With Me?!?	41
17 Equality	43
18 What If Black Girls Knew...?	45
19 It's Not Your Fault!	47
20 The Lion's Den	49
21 Better, Not Bitter!	51

Foreword

In a day and time when women are suffering from low self-esteem and are questioning their God-given value, it is absolutely essential that there are resources to counteract the debilitating effects of this toxic culture.

To this end, God is raising voices: authors, artists and thought leaders who are addressing the attack on womanhood. Maureen is one of these vessels.

This amazing poetic collection is absolutely a welcomed tonic for a toxic culture. Maureen Thompson has taken the skill of a wordsmith and merged it with a divine mandate to empower this generation of broken women.

The content and spirit of "A Girl's Must-Have Pearls" brings the wisdom of God to girls and women who may otherwise live a lifetime without knowing their actual worth.

This collection is so unique in its essence. It is entertaining, informative, inspirational, motivational and introspective all at the same time. Maureen is clearly ordained to bring her artistic gift to this generation to accomplish healing and redirection.

This collection is truly a gem for girls of all ages. As you dive into the spirit of this work, allow God to enlighten, empower and to elevate your self-estimation.

RC Blakes

Acknowledgements

A HUGE thanks to my lifelong friends for nearly 50 years, Josie and Fiona, for being my enthusiastic, personal cheerleaders throughout this writing journey! Love you guys!

A shout out to two fantastic You-tubers that I came across last year, who shone a light on my life so I could reflect on why I thought and behaved the way I did. Now, it makes sense!

Bishop R C Blakes Jr is an empowerment advocate for women, author of books 'The Father-Daughter Talk', 'Queenology' and 'Kingology'. Dr Michelle Daf encourages women into 'feminine rehab' to complement masculine men rather than fight or compete with them. I recommend you tune in…you will learn A LOT!

Finally, but definitely not least, my humble gratitude to my Heavenly Saviour, Jesus Christ, who inspired me to pen these thoughts and emotions that were buried in my soul for so long. Reader, I hope this book inspires you to start your own journey to healing.

Credits

The poem titles "Father Wound" and "Clown with a Crown" are tags often used by Bishop R C Blakes Jnr during his presentations and as such are commonly associated with his ministry. These titles are used with his permission, for which I thank him.

The poem "What if Black Girls Knew" is based on the title "What if a Black Girl Knew", a poem by Dylema Amadi.

Introduction

Growing up in a single mother household, I did not have a positive father presence in my life and convinced myself I didn't really need one, right? Wrong! I knew, even from a young age, that I craved the affection that only a loving father can give to his daughter and the self-worth that can come from that. But there was no dad, so I tried to substitute it in romantic relationships. Big mistake!

The problem was not in having the relationships, but not having love or self-respect for myself, which led to me suffering emotional abuses that left me confused and my heart battered and bruised. Unfortunately, I was also the cause of pain and confusion to others in my life. All stemming, I now believe, from the absence of a father in my life and the rejection of my Father in heaven.

When I became a Seventh-day Adventist Christian in 1992, I realised that the emptiness I had felt for so long was because I didn't know God the Father and how much He loved me. Sounds cliché I know, but I wish I had known this as a young, fatherless, and naïve Black girl, searching for something to fill this huge void that I felt.

I pray these poems promote a higher perception of self-worth to help you, Reader, avoid the consequences and pain of low self-esteem and move on to accept the higher love offered by Jesus Christ.

1 - The Golden Afro

(Disclaimer: I wrote this poem over 10 years ago, just as the afro was making a resurgence, so it might seem moot now. But this is my first book so it should start with my first poem! Also, I am not saying that Black women should not style their hair in the ways mentioned below. No, no, no! Please put down those rocks you are looking to fling at my head! My aim is to arrest the decision-making process so women can reflect on why they are doing it, to ensure they are operating from a level of self-acceptance, not self-loathing.)

She who wears a wig or weave,
Or plaits, or presses or relaxes with ease,
Doth shun her destiny like Mother Eve,
And listens to fables and is deceived.

She holds that beauty does only belong
When hair is straight and shiny and long.
And in this error, she persists and prolongs
The agony of those who would be strong
To resist the tide of guilt and shame:
And, loudly, the beauty of Afro proclaim!

But they shrink and retreat into a cloudless ether,
Like a glorious afro in misty weather.
Who told you that you are not worth a name,
If your hair and the softness of a lamb are the same?

My brothers, alas, I have heard you profess
That the 'sistas' lack class and in beauty are less.
You turn your back and this - worst of all –
Say the afro is 'ugly' and 'unprofessional'!

Who told you that we are not of worth,
When the Lord Himself who made heaven and earth,
Created Adam & Eve in the image of He?
What makes you think we don't look like she?

God makes no mistakes and is like no other,
For out of one colour came every man's mother.
And the God who made the straight, shiny, and long,
Is the same who ordained the soft, curly, and strong.

Our value is not based on what we see,
But in the knowledge of God's love for 'haarrlll a we'!*
For no matter our shape, height, hue or location,
We can all bask in the glow of His adoration.

So, my sisters who dare to hold themselves pure,
And against ignorance, malice and deceit endure,
Beauty may be in the eye to behold,
But in the sight of our Creator, the afro is pure gold!

2 - Whoa! Wait...What?
(Yes, unfortunately, this actually happened in my school!)

He gleefully yelled as he walked through the door,
"Hello there, wh___e!" to the girl that he saw.
Stopped dead in my tracks, 'Did he just say what he said?'
That girl just laughed and cried back "Hey, Fred!"

Hackles raised high, I rounded and asked,
"Do you know that boy-child that just sauntered past?!"
"Oh yeah, he's my friend. It's ok, he's just teasing."
I counted to 10...as I slowed down my breathing!

Did she not know? Why could she not see?
That was not friendship; far below her was he.
What kind of world gets a girl to believe
That an insult is love and not know she's deceived?

They're watching the videos that demean who they are:
Young girls shaking booty to end up a star.
The 'B' word is fly in the MTV sphere,
But the wisdom of mum they just don't want to hear.

They think they're in charge, holding men in their palm,
Not knowing these men are out to do harm.
Girl power is fine, but they must know instead
That the power is not their body...it's what's inside their head.

I burned hot within, whilst acutely aware
That the pain of old insults was starting to flare.
But I kept my cool (I looked so serene!)
And said very firmly to this misinformed teen,

"Don't let any boy talk to you that way!
He's not your friend, but *you* are his prey!
Look him in the eye the next time he's seen,
And say 'Get gone, joker! I'm no wh__e...I'm a queen!'".

3 - I Wish I Knew When I Was You

I wish I knew when I was you,
That water was clear and not actually blue!
That stars don't care what you think, do or say,
They're just gonna shine, no matter what may.

I wish I knew when I was you,
That roses are red, while violets are blue.
But what a boy said was not meant to be true,
And as King Mongtut* raged, "It's a false lie!" too.

How I wish I knew when I was you,
That boys are just mean and out to hurt you.
They play with your heart and when they are done,
They bury you in the garden, like a dog with a bone!

Then they scamper away sniffing out the next pleasure,
All the while knowing that you are buried treasure.
Another tracks your scent, and he starts to dig,
But the mutt comes back like a greedy pig!

*The name of the King of Siam from the film "The King and I" starring Yul Brynner and Deborah Kerr

Licking his lips from the meal he's just had,
He sees off the digger – Oh that mongrel! That cad!
"Hey dog, that's mine! Move on, brother, be gone!"
Then he sniffs you once over… and again buries you alone!!

I wish I knew when I was you,
That I didn't have to accept another's value.
I was not meant to be licked, and slobbered over,
Then left in the ground by that mongrel rover!

I didn't have to accept to be treated like trash,
Or buried in dirt like a cold fire's ash.
God's heart was breaking while I languished in earth,
So He knelt down beside me to tell me my worth.

"You're far above rubies." God said to me:
As He lifted me up to be who I should be.
He said I was created as a bright star to shine.
"I am your Redeemer. I've called you by name. You are Mine".

He wiped off the dirt that he washed with His tears,
For I was stained with neglect after all those cruel years.
He took off the rags I had bound round so tight,
And gifted a robe of salvation, snow white.

He placed on my head a crown of pure gold,
As His journey of love to find me, He told.
"When I heard you cry and your hot tears did flow,
No mountain was too high and no valley too low.

I crossed raging oceans and hot deserts I trod
To settle your ransom, which I paid with my blood.
You must see I love you, for far did I roam
To find you, my child, and to bring you back home."

I cried with relief and knew from that day
That the Lord took my shame and my sorrow away.
Down in that pit, I really wish I knew
That God TRULY loved me…especially when I was you!

4 – Black Pearl

Her passage is plagued with idols of earth
That do not reflect her value or worth.
Double-tied with weights of oppression and shame
That threaten to capsize her mission and name,
She battens the hatches and gazes above
To keep in her vision God's rainbow of love.

Bowed down with burdens and soaked through with tears,
She moves on with purpose through all of her years.
She sees not her future far ahead in time,
But knows that God's path is set in the sublime
Providence of His will at every stride.
So, she presses ahead, close by His side.

A woman of valour found not in life's ease,
Or in parties of pleasure in cities that seize
The overworked senses and debauch the mind.
This woman of valour…where can we find?
She is not found in measures of length,
But in crucibles of pressure that bring forth strength.

Deep in the mud of rejection and fear,
The irritants of life mould this precious sphere.
Ground down by careless, ignorant philosophy,
Time tells the material is not what they thought it would be.
Better than gold and all the jewels of the world,
Is the magnificent beauty of the rare black pearl.

5 – Clown with a Crown*

Why are you touching me there?
Why are you touching me anywhere?
Who gave you permission? Did I say?
Why are you mauling me anyway?!?

Don't you understand how much I'm worth?
I am not like a lump of earth
For you to paw and poke and prod,
Like some perverse toddler playing with mud!

What do you mean you don't need a job?
Do you expect me to marry a slob?
What example for our son would you be
If all you do is play on the Wii??

Oh! You're not ready to settle down?
Then why with me are you messing around?
My time is much too precious to waste
On someone who's just looking to taste.

*Pastor R C Blakes Jr uses this title to describe immature men (jokers) who engage in superficial relationships with women without offering them any real substance, e.g. marriage, loyalty, sexual fidelity, etc. as 'kings' (committed, quality men) would.

What made you think that you had a right
To manhandle a diamond that was in your sight?
Just because I caught your eye,
Doesn't mean you can afford to buy.

Do you see the stars above that shine?
Now *that's* the destiny that is mine.
Chosen as a bride for a king,
I am NOT some joker's plaything!

Crafted from DNA knit in a bone,
Designed to reign with my king on his throne.
Love and honour God gemmed in my crown:
I was made for a king, not for you, Clown!

6 – Queens of Colour

Red skin, brown skin, black skin, or blue.
Yellow skin, white skin, orange-flecked too!
Do you believe that one colour is better?
Or teach little girls that it really doesn't matter?
Is success in this world to be based on our sight?
Is there only one colour that seems to be right?

As a young girl I would see on TV,
That the most beautiful girls just didn't look like me!
With pinky-pale skin and hair shiny and long,
They bore into my psyche, deep-rooted and strong.
So, alone in my room, on my head I would wear
My black, long-sleeved cardy…and flicked it like hair!

On TV today (you know that it's true!)
It's only black girls that don't use shampoo!
The tights that are made come in skin colour or nude:
Now, I don't mean to moan…but that's just plain rude!
I've checked many times and when I'm undressed,
I'm still in the shade of which my God did bless!
(BTW, I AM nude, and the tights still don't match, but we'll move on!)

How is it that light skins want an even suntan
That turns their skin brown, but they don't want to BE black, man?
What on earth is going on (you know this ain't right!)
When black girls bleach DNA, just so they can be light?
If diversity is celebrated, then how can it be,
That I want to look like you, and you want to look like me?

In this age of enlightenment (please excuse the pun!),
Is beauty based on the shade furthest from the sun?
In 6000 years, where is it that you find
That women are praised for the beauty of their mind?
So in our quest for affirmation, as we're searching to unearth it,
We swallow bilge from profiteers that tell us that "You're worth it!"

What colour was Father Adam or beautiful Mother Eve?
Did God have a preference for the colour of the sleeve
That He bound around His creation when He made them from the earth?
Tell me, if you really can, which colour is of most worth?
Is the golden sun of more value than the deepest, dark blue sea?
To be of any value to you, what colour then should *I* be?

Listen to me carefully now, you know I speak the truth:
Eve and Sarah were magnificent, but so were Zipporah and Ruth.
There were only 8 soggy souls that came forth from the ark of the flood.
So why value only the colour of the skin, when we're all from the same red blood?
Daughters are we from the Noadic line, is the Bible's full revelation.
They handed down their DNA to every generation.

We are all separated sisters, fighting against the tide
Of manipulation, mutilation, misogyny, and pride.
Many are the wonderful women from nations of every hue.
You're no better than me, my sis, and I'm no better than you.
Now, let us take a stand so we can learn from what we've seen;
That the only shade of supreme value is God's royal colour of 'Queen'.

7 - Baby Girl

You are so beautiful, so exquisitely formed,
You take my breath away!
The crowning glory of our love for God,
I am lost for words to say.

How is it that you came from me,
So awesome and wonderfully made?
How is it possible that God used we
As the cradle in which you were laid?

I cannot tell of what I did right
To deserve such a gift as you.
I only know that my heart feels to burst
With a love so strong and true.

To wrestle with lions, fight tigers and bears,
I was willing to right from the start.
There's nothing in this life I wouldn't risk for you –
I would give you my very heart!

So, it grieves me more than you'll ever know
To see you mistreated this way.
That man has no idea of your value
When on you his brute hands he does lay!

I died inside every time I saw
Your greying eyes hiding the sun.
"I'm so clumsy…" you faltered, "…I tripped and fell."
Then he phoned and called you "Hun."

I burned with rage when he drew you close
With kisses so tender and sweet.
I cried in my soul when I saw you the next day
And you could barely stand on your feet!

"Leave him!" I begged, "He'll kill you, you know!"
And sobbed as I slumped to the floor.
"You don't understand! I love him so much!"
And you got up and showed me the door.

My aching heart freezes each time the phone rings,
Dreading to hear the words said,
"Is this the mother of daughter so-and-so?
I'm so sorry to tell you…she's dead!"

What a destiny for a mother to have
To bear in this cruel, dark world!
There should never be a time and a place
That a mother outlives her little girl.

How does this happen, why can't they see
How precious they are in God's sight?
Why don't they know that every man should have
Knowledge according to God's light?

He that loves his wife, loves himself,
For no man does hate his own flesh.
Will a man break his arm? Or slap out his own eye?
No way, for the two are one mesh.

Our Father in heaven gave the example to show
How a man treats the wife of his youth.
"Husbands love your wives, even as Christ loved the church." *
Now *that* is the gospel truth!

I pray every day for you, daughter, to see
That you were not minted to live
This soul-tie of bondage to a demon in pants,
For Christ died for you, His love to give.

Because you are so beautiful, so exquisitely formed,
I know exactly what to you I should say.
My sweet baby girl, pack your bags and come home,
Before that devil takes your breath away!

*Ephesians 5:28, 29

8 – Daddy's Girl

(What every girl should hear! Not sure why, but I imagined this dad speaking in an American southern accent. I'm thinking Matthew McConaughey…sounds very comforting in my head!)

My Daddy one night did say to me that, "Not all men are dogs.
But the ones that are low-down nuff feral, will sniff around you like hogs.
So, keep your heart on lockdown closed but your eyes full open wide,
Cos some of these trufflers are sneaky bad and will come at you from the side!

They vine-step in so smoothly, full of all sweetness and light:
'Mmm girl, you look so fine today! Can I take you out tonight?'
They sweating you hard daily, girl, but keep your head on straight,
And tell that truffling porker that he'll just have to wait!

Tell him you have morning classes, and you'll meet for lunch instead.
I know that's not the meal he's thinking; he's wanting breakfast in bed!
'Oh baby, I can't wait that long! It's got to be tonight.
Don't you love me, honey? You know I'll treat you right.'

He oils himself in closer, preparing to spring the trap.
'You know that you my wifey!' Now don't you dare fall for that pap!
Guys use that line all the time, you know," my Daddy wisely did say.
"They know what lonely girls long to hear, so they know what rap to play.

Don't be fooled so easily by what a man has said.
Use your brains, my baby girl, to keep one step ahead.
From the abundance of his heart, his mouth will surely speak.
Tell him you can't see him tonight. See if he calls you next week!

Don't give yourself so easily to a man that flashes cash.
Armani suits and Bentleys don't mean he won't treat you like trash.
A joker might try to holler you to meet at a fast eatery.
He slyly thinks he doesn't have to try. 'Ha, I'll get this one for free!'

Some pimps will drool on your pictures that on social media they find.
If you want to be taken seriously by men, then don't take shots of your behind!
If someone's wife you intend to be, then dress for a husband to meet.
Don't squeeze into clothes that show your DNA and look like you're walking the street!

Believe it or not there are good men out there, looking for love that is true.
But if you're surrounded by jokers who are not, how will they ever find you?
Mercedes Benz men are driving around searching for a permanent space.
But they'll keep driving past you, cos all they can see is a broken-down Skoda* on base!

When you meet a man and he loves you true, he'll make it so very plain.
His conduct will show that he values you, not knowingly causing you pain.
His boundless respect is abundantly clear for he will not use any stealth.
And how will you know that he honours you? He will keep his hands to himself!

My job as your dad is to show you how to navigate your way through this life.
For you to get the husband you deserve, you have to look like his wife.
Fathers protect their precious daughters from wolves who look like sheep:
You don't want a man who will eat up your life, but someone who wants you to keep.

So, get schooled, my daughter, and continue to strive to be the best you can be.
Be wise, but don't worry 'bout those prairie hound-dogs, cos they ain't gonna get past me!"

*Skodas used to have a bad rep back in the day! I think they're quite cool now though, so no hard feelings, please!

I listened intently to what my dad said to protect me from pain in this world.
I kissed him goodnight, said, "I love you, Dad!", so glad I am this Daddy's girl.

9 – Father Wound

How can it be that a man you don't know
Can hurt you when he's not around?
How do you scream from a pain deep within
And no-one can hear any sound?

They look in your face while they chatter away,
Not seeing a smile that is bare.
Why can't they see that you're wounded and chained
To a man who just isn't there?

What is this longing that tugs in my heart
For a man that will never be mine?
Why did he leave me to carry the shame?
Why did he leave me behind?

Groping around for a lifeline of love
That I know his shadow can't throw.
Fronting indifference to lack that is plain,
I tread where no angel should go.

Desperately dwelling in a house made of straw,
I think I've got nothing to lose.
But I find out too late from that old camel's back

I've made hay from my own 'father bruise.'

Guys don't respect a girl with no dad
To warn her and make himself clear.
They drink deep and long, and then throw the can back,
As they reach for the next brand of beer.

Why did I stay when I knew well to run
From a pain that my father did start?
How could I cling to the lie that he told
When he threw down and stamped on my heart?

The years that I wasted not knowing my worth
And settling for crumbs from the table.
The tears that I cried as I shackled myself
To that rusty 'dad issues' label.

I wish I had known that my heavenly Father
Had loved me before I was born.
I wish that I knew how He gave up His life,
While my earthly sub put me to scorn.

No greater love has a man that is true,
Than to lay down his heart and to give
The best of himself for his lost, lonely child,
So the best of their life they can live.

This is what Christ did for me and for you,
To show us how much we are worth.
He poured out His love that is way beyond reach
Of the best of the fathers on earth.

The wounds from her daddy will sting for a while
When a girl knows that he doesn't care.
But nothing can separate a girl from the love
Of a Father who'll always be there!

10 – A Good Man

A good righteous man that is sent to you from God,
Doesn't need to be handsome or have a great bod!
He is much slow to anger, not full of man's wrath.
And easy to cherish when walking God's path.

He is eager to please you and not cause you pain.
An abundance of blessings on you he will rain.
He'll keep his eye single to love you on task,
Forsaking all others, not wearing a mask.

Not caring for games, he will honour his queen,
A quality woman he'll see as supreme.
Far above rubies, he treasures his prize
As one to be desired to make a man wise.

Committed to purpose he'll beat out his way,
Allowing God's grace to lead day by day.
Submission is key to this man God ordains,
For no fear of betrayal his queen entertains.

Anointed as king, he follows God's mission,
And covers his woman with love and compassion.
She need never fear that his love will depart,
For the two are as one and she lives in his heart.

This man can be yours for the truth is so plain:
If you follow God's plan, he will heal all your pain.
Forgive yourself true and forget all your woe:
Just trust that God loves you because He said so.

If bitterness roots it will rob you of rest.
When the king comes your way, you will not be your best,
For your past fear will freeze you and your anger will slay
Any man who dares try take your dragon away.

So, pledge to be happy and self-love pursue,
For no man can cherish an untameable shrew.
Be as wise as an owl and as sweet as a dove
To receive that good man sent from heaven above.

11 – Long Live the Queen

(I wrote this one as I watched the televised funeral for HM Queen Elizabeth II in 2022. End of an era!)

Our Queen is now dead, but long live the queen
Who carries herself so calm and serene.
An image of grace, so regal and fine,
Liz showed us the way to capture a man's mind.

Elizabeth II was born for her role,
Cementing her honour in man's deepest soul.
Commanding respect with her smile and a wave,
No man in her presence would dare misbehave!

She gathered our hearts with no taint of disdain,
And proved that a monarch with wisdom could reign.
A woman of steel wrapped in a warm, velvet glove;
No wonder her subjects could easily love.

Her standard was high, and she brooked no reproach:
Men quaked in their boots, her throne to approach!
But they left with heads high like a stag on a veld,
For the favour she showed and the peace that she held.

She walked with finesse the fine line of fame,
Being gracious to friends and her foes all the same.
Constant through purpose given her of God,
An example to women, her long road she trod.

We all have our mission, our path to unfold,
And this great Queen of England was a pattern to hold.
Don't let men tell you that women are weak,
Or stumble and fumble, their approval to seek.

As queens ourselves we must hold our hearts high,
Not low to the ground where clowns love to lie.
Not so high as to be out of sight,
But borne at a level that makes a man right.

With conscious dignity we must make it plain
That no man is welcome who is zealous for pain.
As women of virtue, we must be seen
As royal by birthright, so…LONG LIVE THE QUEEN!

12 – Mum

Why did we fight when there was no need;
Her counsel of love I just had to heed.
Her own road behind her, she saw my path plain;
I didn't have to walk that same path of pain.

But, of course, I knew better. Who was she to say
I had no wisdom! No respect did I pay!
I walked on regardless of where she had been.
Nothing could she teach me, for I was 17!

Time was not delayed for me to learn the truth.
That's why God made mums for naïve youth.
Ignore mum's advice and surely you will fall,
For her wisdom is experience and knowledge for us all.

One person's pain does not have to be your gall,
And I wish I had listened to history's call.
My mum was so right, and I will never doubt
That her love was the stone over which we fell out.

For most it's a stumbler, for others the lift
To that next level chapter which opens the gift.

Obedience in life to the commandments of God
Is the duty we learn from those who have trod.

The first mother failed us and handed down shame,
But the choices we make, on ourselves we must blame.
We stand now as sinners, but salvation can come
Through pearls that are given by our Father through our mum.

13 – Don't Get Caught a' Bush!
(The English translation of 'bush' would be the bike-shed!)

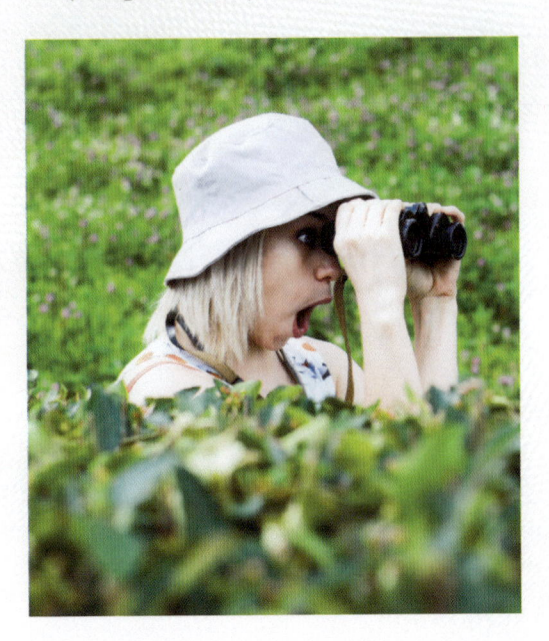

My Bajan friend was always saying.
To leave school she was in a rush.
What one lesson would she take with her?
She said, "Don't get caught a' bush!"

We raised a brow, then thinking hard,
We asked, "Which teacher said that?"
She rolled her eyes, sighed, "No teacher…my mum!"
We looked at each other, "Say Whaaat?"

Well, I never heard it said before,
So I whispered back in a hush.
"What did Mrs Brown mean to say
When she said, 'Don't get caught a' bush'?"

"I don't know what she really meant,
But to ask I never did push.
All I know is it rings in my ears,
'Don't get caught a' bush!'"

We mused a while, then triumphantly said,
"It means when we walk in the park,
To keep an eye on the time that it shuts
So we don't get left in the dark!"

We kinda knew that it didn't make sense,
But it took us a number of years
For life to rock and roll us around
And realise Mother Brown's fears.

We heard of girls who got spread abroad
Getting fame that never was good.
They started the year, then were out the back gate
As they entered teen motherhood.

"Ah" we said, "So that's what she meant!"
As we piously shook our small heads.
Envisioning bushes shaking around
As teenagers made their own beds.

We did not know the time was yet near
To stumble off our high path.
The variation was the time of our fall,
For there's no difference in Satan's wrath.

So, we set on the road that came to our feet,
Not reading the signs on the map.
With rose-tinted glasses we skipped gaily on
And fell headlong straight into a trap!

This trap was a game invented by men,
Designed to keep us off guard.
We followed their trail that led us right up
To that bush in Satan's back yard.

Three unplanned babies with no man in sight,
Invited this bush escalation.
Two miscarriages, and one marriage from hell,
Cemented Ma Brown's revelation.

Why do old women speak truth that they know,
But not make it clear what they mean?
How can young women learn games to avoid
If they can't read the rules in-between?

How do old women see far into life
To warn us of things yet to come?
Why do young women despise their advice,
Disdaining to eat any crumb?

The bush was not a location of space,
But decisions that were our own making.
Getting caught was an outcome of broken esteem
That laid us all bare for the taking.

Ma Brown was right to warn her young girl
To avoid the cruel workings of men.
School might be useful to learn ABCs
But there's much more to life than the pen.

We've come out the wiser, though battered and bruised,
As we scrape off the thorns from life's brush.
We will never forget now that wise Bajan mother
Who said, "Don't get caught a' bush!"

14 – Betrayed

I thought I was wise (twas in my own eyes!).
No prey would I be! (I just couldn't see).
Where did I go wrong? And why for so long?
How did I get led? I'm scratching my head!

The first time I saw that this would be war,
I pardoned the crime, but took not the time
To analyse why the boy made me cry.
I knew what he did, but reason I hid.

I thought it was right to cover my sight
To gain what I craved; this 'love' that he gave.
He twisted my head with lies that he fed.
I ate them up whole and swallowed my soul.

I knew right from wrong, but self-esteem gone,
I lowered the bar and stayed in the car.
Then when I got used and battered and bruised,
I blamed it on he, but found it was me!

Betrayed from the start by my foolish heart,
I cannot deny my standards did fly.
And left broken down, I gave up my crown,
And settled for less than my God would bless.

It's easy to say, that that joker should pay,
But my freedom to choose puts paid to that ruse.
No chains did God give to force me to live
Outside of His will, for He loves me still.

My heart had to break for God to remake
This version of me that was meant to be.
I'm on higher ground, new grace I have found
To let go my past and embrace God at last!

So, value the prize you see in God's eyes,
For he's looking at you with love strong and true.
You must release strife to live your best life,
And believe that you can when you follow God's plan.

15 – A Good Man Lost

He tried so hard my love to win,
But damaged was I, and cold within.
I feared myself below his grasp,
And dared my heart to break the clasp.

I pledged myself to test the line
To see if he was really mine.
I threw the glove to start the fight,
And watched as love limped out of sight.

The fool I was, I thought it well
To tell his faults and made it hell
For him to try and bring me close.
My independence I did boast!

He showed me well his love was true
But I dug in and played the shrew.
His heart I rung and squeezed the juice,
Until, at last, I shook him loose.

The madness is, I didn't see
Till decades late, how good was he!
He never once did make me doubt
If his love for me was shared without.

To spend his time with me he would,
Just like a good man always should.
He shared his heart, his love was deep.
He made it plain I was to keep.

But plagued with fear, I would not believe,
And that Snake around my heart did weave
A vice that gripped and choked the life
I could have had if I'd let go strife.

My brokenness just could not see
The man I had could love just me.
So, I pushed him away before he did me,
And live to regret my insanity!

But God's cleansing blood removes all stain
Of damage done and deepest pain.
That battle is lost, but now I see
That God is not yet done with me.

The pain of past mistakes must heal
To show that faith in God is real.
To take it back I cannot do,
But God has made my heart anew.

Content alone, but if I'm blessed
To love again, I do confess
I'll honour God and know the cost,
And never again make a good man lost.

16 – What is Wrong with Me?!?

Why did I let that farce go on? I laugh about it now.
I tried to make that old silk purse from strips of an old mad cow!
I knew it in my soul! I knew!! I knew he'd do me harm!
But zombified by his handsome face, I swooned into his arms.

The problem was he pulled them back and watched me crash to the floor!
I said, 'My bad!' as I cricked my neck and hobbled back up for more!
He played the flute, and I asked how high to jump for him I should?
He strolled ahead and I scampered behind like a love-hungry puppy would.

His birthday came and I baked a cake, convinced I'd seal the deal.
He limply said 'Oh thanks. That's…nice.' and crushed my soul for real!
Yet, undeterred, convinced I'd be the one to make him change,
I laid down on his altar of shame and gave the brute free range!

What makes it worse is I look back now and knew I'd seen the light.
I hated how he made me feel; I knew he just wasn't right!
'What's wrong with you?' I asked myself. 'You know you're better than this!'
'You might be right, but he's the first guy I don't have to bend down to kiss!'

I rolled my eyes and kissing my teeth*, refused to speak to me for days.
I crossed the street, my reflection to scorn, upset with my stupid ways!
We made up, though, when he had the nerve to say it just wouldn't work.
Why do men want to test you out but commitment they just want to shirk?

I said, 'That's fine.' My heart didn't break, but I was miffed that I didn't say,
'You're tall, my brother, and handsome to boot, but your kiss I no like anyway!'
So, what's the lesson, I asked myself? Just what *was* wrong with me?
I didn't ask God to choose from the heart and not from what I could see.

---

*Jamaican colloquial term for a sound of derision made with the mouth. A more emphatic 'tsk', you might say.

17 - Equality

Glorious were the days of old
When ladies were quaint, and men were bold.
Everyone knew and kept their place,
And chivalry was high amongst the race.

Men opened doors and gave up their seat,
To show their respect was full and complete.
Women, though viewed as the frail "weaker sex",
Were cherished as flowers with much circumspect.

They kept the home and children ruled,
To hold the line and keep them schooled.
Men worked hard to keep families fed,
As they battled the soil for their daily bread.

But I hear you cry that abuse was rife,
And women had no joy of life.
Wreckage of souls was wide and high,
And the 'Good old days' was just a lie!

Misuse was made of God's Eden plan
When creating the home for woman and man.

Mutual respect and trust was the key
To eternal, Edenic equality.

That traitorous snake put a spoke in the wheel,
And sold them a lie for the love that was real.
Adam's wife was thrown under the bus,
And settled the score for the rest of us.

To redress the balance we've gone way too far,
By cramming good men in that specimen jar.
How high can we go, if, for women to rise,
We humiliate, denigrate and all men despise?

I wish we would live out the life that was true,
And give back to mankind its godly value.
Two equal wrongs don't make it a right
To justify putting all men out of sight.

Our roles were given as suited us best,
So all of mankind would be equally blessed.
Division of labour is never a sin
When all are united, one goal to win.

If hand and foot were created the same,
The body its purpose would never proclaim.
But both work together, that mountain to climb,
And the teamwork it brings is supremely sublime!

So the next time you're told that men are just dirt,
Remember that God did make man from the earth!
Sunshine and rain are both needed we know,
But without the good soil, no flower would grow!

18 – What if Black Girls Knew...?

What if black girls knew…?
That beautiful eyes don't have to be blue.
And wrapped up in an ebony embrace
Is a perfect reflection of God's loving grace.
What if black girls knew?

What if black girls knew…?
That their shimmering shade is the perfect hue
To glitter like diamonds unveiled in the light,
That are made all the brighter against deepest night.
What if black girls knew?

What if black girls knew…?
That their hair is their glory, as God said it true.
Its versatile texture demands true respect
As it crosses all boundaries of strand circumspect.
What if black girls knew?

What if black girls knew…?
That all of their sisters are different shades too.
That flowers the same were not meant to be,
For beauty in all we were meant to see.
What if black girls knew?

What if all the girls knew…?
That the colour of skin does not define you.
That being black or white is the same,
And the one thing that matters is having God's name.
What if all the girls knew?

19 – It's Not Your Fault!

It's not your fault he looked your way.
It's not your fault you trusted him.
It's not your fault he took your innocence away.
It's not your fault! You trusted him!

How could you know the depravity
That lurked within his mind?
Why would you fear a family friend
Who closed the door behind?

You didn't do a single thing
To cause his star to fall.
You were too young to understand.
You did no wrong at all!

You live your life with guilt and shame,
Replaying every scene.
"If I'd done this. If I'd said that."
It was your fault, you mean.

Don't blame yourself for what he did,
There's nothing you could have done.
He snaked his way around your home;
There was nowhere to run.

You must not own the guilt of one
Who put your life in shade.
You must not close the door to hope;
You must not live afraid!

If you have let your anger spread
To sear a hole in your heart,
Our God can soothe that fiery tide
To give a brand new start.

Forgiveness is the only way
To set your spirit free.
So let him go to release your heart,
And be who God made you to be.

20 - The Lion's Den

Naïve in worldly ways of men,
She hears the call from a lion's den.
Convinced that, as the prize, she'd win,
She boldly dares to jump straight in.

He gazes up and down awhile,
And perceives she's unaware of guile.
No schooling she received to keep
Her heart intact and mind from sleep.

Her mother failed to make it clear,
And whisper wisdom in her ear.
For in the wild we often see
The game is played by more than he.

He pads around her like that cat:
With soothing words, he lays her flat.
The death grip tight, she gasps for air,
And prays the Lord her soul to spare.

God hears the plea and thunders down,
His lamb to place on higher ground.

No longer prey to be a feast,
She's free and flees the fearsome beast.

The thief comes not but for to steal
The lambs of God, and feast for real.
As men are moved by Satan's frown,
They spoil the girl, her soul to drown.

But scars will heal and lesson learned,
She'll trust the Lord for whom she yearned.
His path, although not monster-free,
Will lead her to eternity.

21 – Better, Not Bitter!

Women tossed aside by men,
Will burn inside and think of when
The tide will turn and vengeance rain
On sandy shores that caused them pain.

They plot and scheme to make men pay
For the miserable lies from that scornful melee,
Where boys kissed girls and made them cry
By twisting their hearts to bleed them dry.

As Scarlett toyed with simps* of old,
These modern girls are broken bold,
And leave their hearts and souls behind
To wreak revenge on all 'menkind'.

The blasting trump of their battle cry,
Is "If men can do it, then so can I!"
They sally forth in the woeful belief
That counting bodies will bring relief.

*Generally used as an insult to men who are considered submissive to women who are not interested in them anyway and are just using them to pay their bills, buy clothes, jewellery, etc. (Reference to the treatment of men by Scarlett O'Hara from the book and film, "Gone With The Wind").

Who wins the war with a crown to yield
Before the soldiers have fought in the field?
And who gains victory in the wrestlings of life
By cutting their throat with the enemy's knife?

A woman's path is strewn behind
With shattered dreams and a tortured mind.
In front are stones of impatient haste
That ruin hearts and make lives waste.

Like eyes of cats, they mark a path
That keeps us from the side of wrath.
Living with hate is no life at all,
For growing in grace is destiny's call.

Be grateful that God did not hide
The hazards that are scattered wide,
But in His wisdom gave us tools
To stop us from becoming fools.

Throw not your pearls before the swine,
Then wail as he tramples them behind.
Cast not your troth on the piggy's snout.
If you spot a trotter, then just get out!

Discernment is the key to life,
If you desire to be a wife.
A prize is not an easy gain,
As value is added by toil and pain.

If you desire to be a wife,
Don't place your virtue on a butcher's knife.
For a man must strive to make it clear
That what he desires is precious and dear.

Grounded fruit are a free-for-all.
But a boy will scale up a tree that is tall,
For the challenge to climb is a sought-for task
And the fruit at the top does not have to ask.

Treasure that is earned is a sweet reward,
Like a war that is won with the sweat of the sword.
A woman is won by a man that will fit her,
So, make yourself worthy of better, not bitter!

Printed in Great Britain
by Amazon